INTIMACY

Satisfaction the ultimate goal

By

Wallace B. Learned

Table of Contents

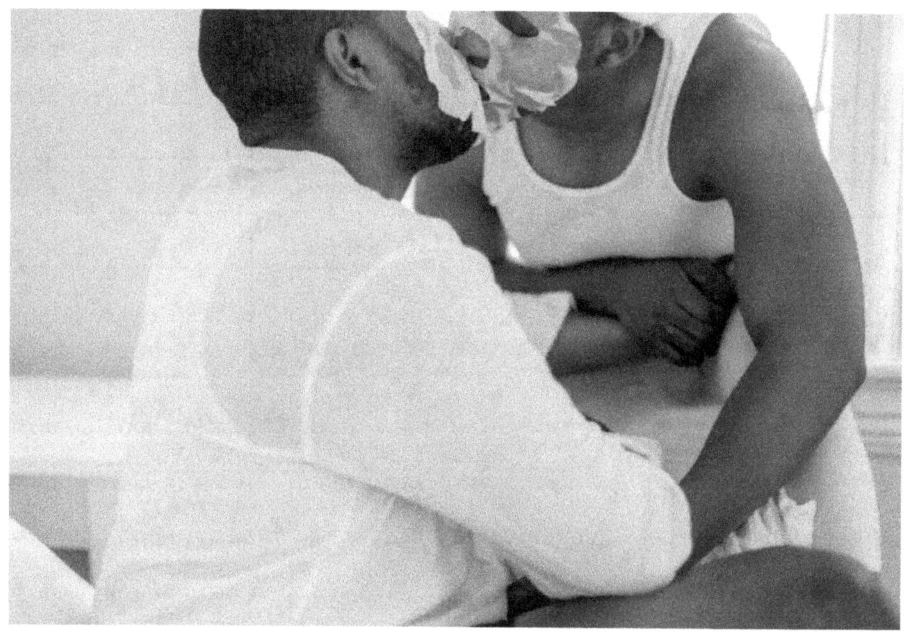

Introduction

Sexual satisfaction is a fundamental aspect of human well-being, yet it is often shrouded in shame, taboo, and misinformation. The book of sexual satisfaction aims to break down these barriers and provide readers with a comprehensive guide to enhancing their sexual experiences and relationships.

Written by experts in the fields of sex therapy and sexual health, the book covers a wide range of topics, from the basics of sexual anatomy and physiology to the intricacies of sexual psychology and the art of seduction. It offers practical advice and strategies for improving communication, building trust, and establishing boundaries in sexual relationships.

The book also explores the role of cultural and societal factors in shaping our attitudes and beliefs about sex, and encourages readers to challenge traditional gender roles and embrace diversity and inclusivity in their sexual experiences. It provides guidance on sexual health, contraception, and sexual dysfunction, empowering readers to make informed decisions about their sexual well-being.

Whether you are single or in a relationship, the book of sexual satisfaction is a valuable resource for anyone looking to improve their sexual experiences and relationships. It is accessible, informative, and empowering, and is sure to make a positive impact on the lives of those who read it.

Through the book's practical advice and insights, readers will gain a better understanding of their own needs and desires, as well as those of their sexual partners. They will learn how to communicate effectively, establish boundaries, and explore new ways of experiencing pleasure. The book also addresses important topics such as consent, sexual orientation, and sexual identity, providing readers with the tools they need to navigate the complex landscape of human sexuality.

What sets the book of sexual satisfaction apart is its focus on holistic sexual health. The authors emphasize that sexual satisfaction is not just about physical pleasure but also about emotional and psychological fulfillment. They encourage readers to explore their own sexuality and embrace their unique sexual identities, while also emphasizing the importance of building strong and healthy sexual relationships.

Overall, the book of sexual satisfaction is an essential resource for anyone looking to improve their sexual experiences and relationships. It provides readers with the knowledge and skills they need to navigate the complexities of human sexuality with confidence and clarity, empowering them to lead more fulfilling and satisfying sexual lives. Whether you are a healthcare professional, a therapist, or an individual seeking to enhance your sexual well-being, this book is a must-read.

Ways to Satisfy A Woman In Bed Like A Pro

Are you trying to find techniques to make ladies happy in bed? If so, you are not by yourself. Many guys are looking for strategies to win over their partners and improve their enjoyment of sex. Fortunately, there are a few straightforward things you can do to ensure your girlfriend is happy.

In this post, I'll give you 17 tried-and-true strategies for getting a lady to like you in bed and crave your company more. Make sure to finish the article in order to comprehend all the minute elements that could have a significant impact on your woman's level of sexual happiness.

17 Ways to Please a Lady in Bed:

Compared to men, women have different wants in bed. Here are the 17 things you must know today if you want to satisfy your woman and make her need more of you sexually.

1. Increase sexual arousal and intimacy

Women and men differ significantly. Before they can appreciate having sex, they need to feel cherished and unique.

Hence, you must first make an extra effort to win her over outside of the bedroom. For instance, you ought to take her out on a special date and engage in flirting with her.

All of these verbal and physical flirtations will contribute to increasing the sexual tension and anticipation needed to heighten the subsequent sexual experience.

She will feel more at ease having sex with you if you can help her feel valued and cherished. She will also be more likely to find the entire process enjoyable.

Thus, always keep in mind that seduction starts outside of the bedroom. She will feel more contented in bed later on if you can make her feel cherished outside of the bedroom.

2. To have satisfying sex, women must engage in foreplay

Many men become frustrated after successfully throwing their woman into bed. They can't wait to start having sex with their favorite women after ripping off their clothes.

This is a serious error because most women prefer to begin slowly and enjoy the foreplay before engaging in sexual activity.

They want you to kiss her, explore her body with your hand, touch a sensitive area of her body, and feel your desire for her. All of them will increase the sexual tension even more and heighten her desire to have sex with you.

Hence, you should concentrate on all the events before to sex if you want to make her happy in bed. Slowing down will increase her desire for you.

3. Harassment

Another thing you may do to make her more enticing while kissing or having sex with her is to use nasty talk.

You just need to verbally communicate how much you want her and whisper all the naughty things you want to do to her. Say, "I want to sniff your neck, suck your nipples, and taste your pussy so bad," for instance.

Alternately, you may assert some power and demand that she perform some immoral acts with you. Saying things like "spread your legs wider, I want to go deeper" or "lift your hip, I want to pound you harder from behind" are examples of what you can say.

Keep in mind to observe her reaction when you use foul conversation with her. You can keep doing it and amp up the sexual tension if she enjoys it or naughty speaks back. This is a really powerful approach to gratify and titillate women in bed.

4. Sexual role-playing fantasy

Role-playing is a great way to spice up the romance in bed.

You can act out any scenario that comes to mind, such as the traditional nurse-patient pairing, a flight attendant and a passenger, an electrician and a housewife, a pizza delivery, etc.

Ask her what her most repulsive sexual fantasy is if you're still stuck for ideas, and role-play that.

Ultimately, role play is crucial for sex because it can liven up the experience and help you develop your sexual confidence.

5. Lickety-Sucky-Bite

You can explore her mouth with your tongue in addition to licking her neck, the area behind her ear, and the inside of her thigh.

You can also lightly bite or suckle on these areas to arouse her and heighten the sexual tension. She might treat you the same way in return.

Her nipples, lower lips, ear, or finger would be suitable areas to delicately suckle or bite. You may even prepare her for oral sex by inserting your finger into her mouth and letting her suck it if you're feeling very seductive.

6. Engage Her Clitoris

When experimenting with her clitoris, there are a few things to bear in mind. First off, because clitoral tissue is so delicate, it's crucial to begin slowly and build up pressure and speed gradually. Second, the clitoris is easy to stimulate with your fingers or a little, soft toy because it is situated at the top of the vulva. Third, it can frequently be helpful to stimulate other areas of the vulva and vagina at the same time because many women find it difficult to orgasm from clitoral stimulation alone.

Start by gently petting the clitoris with your fingers or a squishy object. To find out what she likes, experiment with varied strokes and speeds. Many ladies favor quick, soft strokes. You can accelerate and apply additional pressure as she becomes more arousal. Use a vibrator if she prefers being directly stimulated in the clitoris. Try out several methods and speeds to see what she like.

If you did well, she can be quite turned on and request that you enter her more quickly.

7. Do A Mind-Blowing Oral Sex On Her

It takes expertise, foreplay, and making sure that you both enjoy the experience to give your lover mind-blowing oral sex.

You might start concentrating on their clitoris once they are aroused. To move the clitoris, move your tongue around it or flick it up, down, or side to side. You can write the letters A, O, or I on her pussy with your tongue if you're feeling very naughty.

In addition, you can softly suck on the clitoris with your lips. If she is extremely aroused, you can then softly enter your tongue into her vagina while pointing it forward and performing the in-and-out motion.

You can always stroke her clitoris with your finger while giving her a blow job to make the experience more intense.

8. Employ a deep seated sex position

The male deeply penetrates the woman during the deep penetration sex position, making her feel every part of him inside her. Moreover, this position permits G-spot stimulation, which can cause powerful orgasms.

You must thrust softly and rhythmically at first, then pick up the pace to increase sexual satisfaction.

The Doggy style position, the seashell position, and the cowgirl position are a few examples of sex positions that allow for deep penetration.

Remember to take breaks as needed because the deep penetration sex position can occasionally be physically taxing.

9. Display Dominance And Let Your Wild Side Free

Being dominated in bed can be a way for some women to relinquish control and experience complete relaxation and pleasure. It can also be a method for them to feel closer to their spouse and have a novel and thrilling sexual encounter.

Also, while their spouse is dominating them, they could feel wanted and seductive. For many women, this can be a tremendous turn-on.

You should initiate sex to give your partner the impression that you are the one in charge and they can follow your lead in order to assert authority in bed.

You should also assert yourself more and take charge while having sex. This implies that you should be in control of the sexual experience's tempo, degree of intensity, and general course. Telling your spouse what you like and what you want them to do is another option.

These suggestions should help you exercise power during sex and make sure that both you and your partner are having a great time.

10. Massage her erratically

Being given an erotic massage can make a woman feel very sensuous and personal. A higher level of arousal may result from the near physical proximity, your soft touch, and general state of relaxation.

Her breasts, thighs, and buttocks, for example, are erogenous zones that you can rub and stimulate. To stimulate her clitoris, you can also use your finger, tongue, or sex toys. She will definitely become hot if you do this.

11. Take Her Hair Or Pull It

Women enjoy having their hair grabbed during sex for a variety of reasons. It may be interpreted by others as a sign of your authority and control. That might give them a sexier and more feminine feeling.

Because it makes people feel loved and desired, it can also heighten arousal and pleasure levels.

There are a few various methods you can use to grab a woman's hair while having sex. You can either grab a clutch of hair on either side of her head while licking her neck, or you can grab a handful of hair at the base of her neck.

If you want to up the ante, you could even use a little amount of force to grip her hair as you enter her in a deep penetration sex position. But be careful not to pull too hard or you risk harming her.

12. Use sex toys

Sex toys can produce sensations that are distinct from those that a partner's body can produce, which can cause orgasms to be more intense.

The G-spot is frequently cited by women as the secret to a pleasurable sexual encounter. The G-spot is about 2-3 inches into the vagina on the front wall.

You can use a sex object with a curved or bulbous head to activate the G-spot. The use of G-spot vibrators can aid to deliver targeted stimulation. Once you've identified your G-spot, you can experiment with various strokes and speeds to determine which ones feel most comfortable.

Concentrating on clitoral stimulation is another technique to use sex toys to appease a lady. At the apex of the vulva, there is a sensitive area called the clitoris. Since it can be a significant source of sexual excitement for many women, it is frequently referred to as the "pleasure button." For optimal effect, use the vibrator to stimulate the clitoris while piercing her.

13. Request her preferences

Giving her complete authority during sex entails asking her what she wants to attempt. She is able to indulge in all of her exciting sexual fantasies thanks to this, which also makes her feel loved and cherished.

She might find it fascinating to occasionally be in the position of dominance. She enjoys having the freedom to perform any heinous acts she desires on you. She could be able to roughhouse ride you, force you to taste her pussy, or tie you up and tease you for amusement.

She will likely select the activities that thrill her the most when she has complete freedom, which might directly increase sexual happiness in bed.

14. Dress canine

Ladies prefer the doggie method because it allows them to stoop down in front of you, show off their butts, and allow you to push them from behind. It is a really attractive and subservient move, no doubt.

In order for you to always reach their G-spot when you thrust in, they can also lift their hip a little. And this will cause an intense orgasm for both of you because of the clenched pussy.

She can also continue to move her hip rearward and fuck herself once you're exhausted. She can now embrace her submissive side even more as a result.

Ultimately, due to its rawness and wildness, the doggie style is one of the best sexual positions that can gratify your woman. She has the ability to completely let go and get fucked in a primitive way.

15. Foster A Romantic Ambiance

A woman may feel more emotionally invested in her partner and the scenario when they are in a romantic setting, which may make her feel more sexy.

A woman may also feel more sexually aroused and receptive while in a romantic environment, which may result in a more pleasurable and rewarding sexual experience.

Lighting, music, and scents should all be used to set the tone for a romantic sex session. Aromatherapy using essential oils can aid to further relax and stimulate the senses. Candles, soft light, and sensuous music can help to establish the mood.

Make sure the bed is tidy and prepared for some serious action. It's also crucial to create a pleasant and welcoming physical environment. A traditional way to set a romantic mood is to scatter some rose petals on the bed.

16. Apply deodorant or perfume

There are a few justifications for using deodorant before having sex. First off, it can aid in disguising any potential body odor. This is crucial if you're self-conscious about how you smell or if your spouse has a strong sense of smell.

Second, using deodorant may keep you dry. This is crucial since perspiration during sexual activity might result in body odor and make the experience uncomfortable for both of you.

On the other hand, wearing scent can add to the atmosphere and enhance the sensual nature of the event. The aroma of perfume is extremely seductive to many women.

17. Alter your sexual position.

Adding novelty to sexual activity might help to increase overall enthusiasm and sexual satisfaction. And adopting a new sexual position is the simplest method to accomplish that.

Try something unique instead of always adopting the traditional missionary position, such as the valedictorian position, the flatiron position, or the ballet dancer position. If you and your partner are comfortable with it, you might also decide to incorporate a small amount of BDSM into it.

Also, you can decide where you want to have sex, such as in front of a mirror, in the shower, on the couch, or even at the kitchen table.

It's essential to remember that every woman is unique, and what works for one may not work for another. Communication and consent are also crucial factors when it comes to sexual satisfaction.

1. Foreplay: Most women require more time and stimulation to become aroused than men. Therefore, it's essential to engage in foreplay before any penetrative sex. This can include kissing, touching, oral sex, and using sex toys. The key is to explore what your partner enjoys and to be attentive to her responses.

2. Communication: Communication is key when it comes to sexual satisfaction. You need to communicate with your partner about what she likes and dislikes, what turns her on, and what she needs to reach orgasm. Listening to her verbal and non-verbal cues can help you understand her needs and desires.

3. Clitoral stimulation: The majority of women require clitoral stimulation to reach orgasm. Therefore, it's important to focus on this area during foreplay and sexual activity. You can use your fingers, tongue, or a sex toy to stimulate her clitoris, paying attention to her responses.

4. Experimentation: Trying out new positions and activities can help you discover what your partner enjoys. Don't be afraid to experiment with different positions, sex toys, and activities that she is comfortable with.

5. Relaxation: Many women find it difficult to relax during sex due to stress or anxiety. It's important to create a relaxing environment, with dim lighting, soft music, and a comfortable temperature. You can also try massaging her or engaging in deep breathing exercises to help her relax.

6. Orgasm: While orgasm is not the only indicator of sexual satisfaction, it's essential to make it a priority. You should focus on your partner's pleasure and take the time to help her reach orgasm. This can involve using a combination of clitoral and vaginal stimulation, paying attention to her breathing and moaning, and asking for feedback.

In summary, satisfying a woman in bed involves communication, experimentation, focusing on her pleasure, and taking the time to help her reach orgasm. Remember that every woman is different, so it's essential to listen to her needs and desires and adjust your approach accordingly.

Here are some additional notes on how to satisfy a woman in bed:

- ❖ Build intimacy: Building intimacy with your partner outside of the bedroom can help create a more satisfying sexual experience. This can involve spending quality time together, sharing your thoughts and feelings, and expressing your affection for one another.
- ❖ Pay attention to the entire body: While clitoral stimulation is essential for many women, don't forget to pay attention to the entire body. Kissing, touching, and massaging can be incredibly pleasurable for women, and can help build anticipation for more sexual activities.
- ❖ Use lubrication: Lubrication can make sex more comfortable and enjoyable for women. Even if your partner is naturally lubricated, adding extra lubrication can enhance pleasure and reduce discomfort during sex.
- ❖ Be open-minded: Be open-minded to trying new things that your partner is interested in. This can include different sexual positions, exploring kinks or fetishes, or experimenting with different types of stimulation.
- ❖ Take your time: Rushing through sexual activities can be a turn-off for many women. Taking the time to engage in foreplay, explore different activities, and pay attention to your partner's needs can lead to a more satisfying sexual experience.

❖ Communicate after sex: After sex, it's important to communicate with your partner about what worked well and what could be improved. This can help build trust and intimacy in the relationship, and lead to a more satisfying sexual experience in the future.

Remember, sexual satisfaction is a two-way street. Both partners should feel comfortable communicating their needs and desires, and be willing to work together to create a pleasurable and satisfying sexual experience.

10 Tricks to Always Please a Lady

Most men who wish to fulfill their partners make one of two mistakes: they both take too long and lose the woman's interest, or they enter the relationship too quickly and make her feel rushed or pushed. There's no shame in admitting you have no idea what you're doing, which is why there are innumerable articles, books, and videos on the issue, but they frequently only serve to further confuse you.

To satisfy a lady and, more crucially, keep her seeking you and returning for more, you need to use mind-blowing yet practical approaches both inside and outside of the bedroom. There are commonalities among ladies that you may utilize to your advantage to make her happy in the bedroom even if every woman is unique, or as we like to say at SQL, every woman and every pussy are unique.

Why She's Unhappy in the Bedroom

You must first determine the issue before talking about how to make her feel satisfied in bed. Not all partner dissatisfaction can be attributed to you. She might be experiencing internal conflict that prevents her from finding fulfillment in the bedroom.

More importantly, it's unlikely that the size of your dick is the main factor in her dissatisfaction. Putting too much focus on your size—something you can't change—instead of your skills—which are completely changeable and improvable—is an all-too-common mistake.

You may transform a woman from being dissatisfied to not only being content but yearning for more with a few minor adjustments. Here are a few of the most typical causes of an unhappy partner.

She is desperate for additional psychological ties.

More so than most males, most women have strong connections to their psychological and emotional selves. If you know how to open a woman's psyche, you can make her dripping wet without even taking off her clothes. On the other side, if you don't know what the hell you're doing, you can fully switch her off and make her as dry as the Sahara.

She probably feels unfulfilled in the bedroom as a result of your overemphasis on physical interactions like caressing, kissing, and fucking. Instead of taking the time to encourage her to think about sex and get ready for sexual activity.

She feels ignored.

You might not listen, which is another plausible possibility. Even if it sounds obvious, she might not be content because you haven't been paying attention to her sexual wants and desires. Have you recently declined her request to go on a romantic getaway? Have you declined to use sex toys when she requested them because you preferred "regular sex"?

Whatever the request, she undoubtedly feels unheard and sexually frustrated because her needs haven't been addressed if you repeatedly turned her down. Imagine if she consistently declined your requests for a blowjob despite the fact that you truly wanted one. How could she refuse to help you with this one easy favor? Therefore, if she goes above and above to accommodate your wants, she undoubtedly feels the same way about you and all the requests you turn down.

She feels coerced into having sex.

Very few women want to feel pressured into having sex with someone or putting up with things that are uncomfortable for them. That does not imply that you should disregard your needs.

She won't be satisfied if she feels coerced into having sex or doing specific behaviors (kinks, bondage, anal), which are founded on healthy relationships where both partners feel heard and understood. If you do this, she will eventually grow distant and completely uninterested in sexual activity.

She thinks an ex is being used to compare her.

Because of an ex-partner, you might not ask her for her opinion because you think you already know what she wants and enjoys. Maybe your ex-girlfriend was an expert in the bedroom and taught you how to do all kinds of weird things like 82 different ways to finger a lady till she orgasms.

After breaking up, you tell your new girlfriend everything you've learnt and are prepared to blow her mind! You are disappointed to find that the answer is pitiful and not at all similar to the ecstatic moaning of your ex-girlfriend. Instead of adapting your methods, you dismiss it as merely being rusty and continue to perform the same thing in bed. Each woman is unique, and we cannot emphasize this enough. Your new lover might not respond favorably to what made your ex-partner climax.

She desires more dialogue

It's true that you haven't flat-out refused her requests, but only because you haven't heard them. She isn't sexually fulfilled since you don't talk about sex with her enough!

Nobody actually instructs us on how to talk about sex. When were you expected to learn how to speak about your sex life effectively because sex help books are too clinical or boring and porn is unrealistic? It's difficult to escape, therefore if you want to develop your sex life and sexual communication abilities, read The Best She's Ever Had: Practical Tips and Effective Methods The best-selling book So You're the One She Brags About was created to help guys who experience resolvable sex and relationship issues.

At least twice a week, you should discuss your sex lives with your partner. If you don't, eventually the lust in the bedroom will be suppressed. Her wants might not be satisfied, and neither will yours.

She believes you take sex way too seriously.

Men in as swiftly as possible with as little distractions as possible, treating sex like a military operation. Men out after the job is finished! Sexual activity is meant to be playful, pleasant, and exploratory rather than serious. Your girlfriend's sexual enjoyment and appetite will likely be some of the fatalities if you rush in like it's some type of battleground.

She could not be happy because you have lost sight of having fun, spontaneity, and playfulness since you are so intent on completing the "Dick In, Dick Out" task. Her desire for something else is being caused by the fact that you no longer engage in foreplay or other thrilling and engaging activities in the bedroom.

She doesn't think you feel confident in your sexuality.

Are you certain of your desires for the bedroom? If the answer is no, you're also not willing to appease a lady. If you want to comprehend her sexuality, you first need to understand your own.

Have you ever reacted angrily to an in-room suggestion? Perhaps your girlfriend wanted to play with your ass or give you a rim job, but you rejected her advances and referred to them as "gay." You are being too judgmental in the bedroom if you have denied receiving a prostate massage and anal just because it wasn't something you considered to be heterosexual. For similar reasons, you've probably declined many other pleasurable things that your girlfriend has suggested doing, which makes her feel rejected and dissatisfied.

How to Always Please a Lady

As every woman is unique, if you are aware of her special sweet spot, make advantage of it! If hesitant, try being kind to her while also being kind to yourself because you get to see her naked. Make sure to run a bubble bath and have it hot and ready before she gets home before moving anything into the bedroom. As soon as she exits, assist her with drying off and getting ready by massaging her with oils and lotions.

Don't go into penetration right away. Allow the sexual tension, need, and anticipation to grow until she is almost dragging you inside of her.

Increase interest

For women, great sex begins in the mind. Her body will be interested in sex if you can get her mind interested in it. A lady can be stirred by fantasizing about having sex with you and envisioning your next move. Make her wait; anticipation and perseverance go hand in hand. Wait before you start ripping one other's clothes off or attempting penetration.

You may create suspense by doing the foreplay right. Describe foreplay. Foreplay can be anything at all. Foreplay is anything that makes you and your woman feel sexy. Start as soon as possible rather than later. Well before entering the bedroom, foreplay might start. Send her a suggestive text message after you leave for work in the morning, telling her that you can't wait to see her and that she should be waiting for you in her sexiest bra and underwear.

When you see her, touch her and use plenty of nasty talk—or, as we like to say at SQL, "sexual expression"—to describe her as a sexy little minx (or slut, if she prefers that term—and to promise that you'll do whatever you want with her body tonight.

Before she takes off her clothes, the idea is to get her arouse and become wet. Use her special turn-on to your advantage to make her want to be touched by you.

Boost your abilities

Making up for any shortcomings you may have in the bedroom is a guaranteed method to win your wife over.

Learn how to eat pussy: When you go down on her, stop saying the ABCs. Instead, concentrate your energies on performing her favorite motions. See how she carries herself. Does she appear to be having fun? Ask her if you're unsure. Find out what she prefers: faster, slower, harder, or gentler.

Try anal: While not for everyone, anal can be satisfying for both sexes. If you're trying anal for the first time, go slowly and use lots of water-based lubrication to stay out of difficulties. Instead of just pushing your finger inside and out, stroke it in a circular manner and let her pull you deep inside.

Beautify the bedroom

Asking her to wear something sexy will make things simpler. Tell her all the time how gorgeous she is and how much you want to touch her. Continuous encouragement is essential! Make her feel special as well as sexy.

By planning your ideal night together, you might encourage each other to experiment with various fantasies and sex positions. Ask her to write down her ideal night and then do the same. What time will the evening start? Which postures does she prefer? She wants an oral or an anal? What is required for her to be completely content in every way? Give her whatever she wants once you've learned. Make sure you are specific and vivid while describing what you want from her so that you don't ignore your own enjoyment.

Why not have an evening of role playing while we're talking about fantasies? It's not everyone's cup of tea, but if you think the bedroom is missing something, pretend to be a seductive student or teacher, bad girl or cop, vampire or vulnerable maiden, or whatever desire you or she might have. Be open-minded and willing to hear or share anything that happens in the bedroom.

Try a dominance and submission night if you're not sure where to begin with role-playing. Take control of the space in the bedroom, direct her, and order her to remove her clothing or touch herself. Pick her up and fling her onto the bed or over your shoulder to make things a little harder.

If you're into it, throw in some sex toys. One of the simplest methods to maximize enjoyment and get her drenched is with sex toys. Your must-have sex objects are:

Excellent for clitoral stimulation is the Hitachi Wand

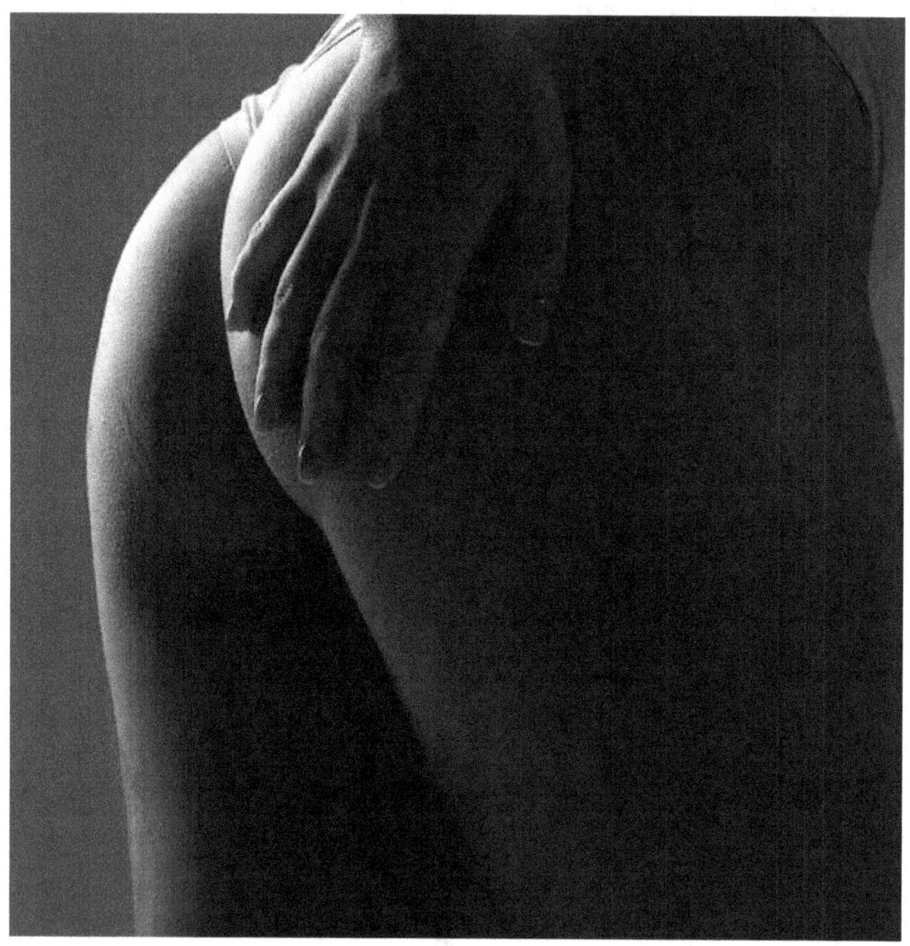

Vibrating Egg: To stimulate the clit and other areas of the vagina, vibrating eggs are available in a variety of sizes and forms. Hold a vibrating egg or a Hitachi Wand to her clitoral region as you penetrate her for more stimulation during sex.

When fucking her, you can turn up the vibrating butt plug to experience the vibrations. She will enjoy this toy if she enjoys anal.

Consider a date instead of

Women need to feel special and attractive, so if you haven't recently taken your spouse out on a date, that might be the reason she's not happy in the bedroom. Don't just take her to dinner and a movie though. Increase the stakes by letting her live a fantasy.

Plan a trip, and organize everything. She shouldn't have to think about anything, so she can relax and have fun. She should have only been thinking about packing her bag and bringing her best underwear. Make it a point to shop before your trip if she doesn't have any.

The Suited Gentleman is the name of this move. Take her to a fine restaurant, dress to impress, and get a luxurious hotel room for the night. Tell her that you've got her tonight and will take care of everything, and encourage her to wear her sexiest bra and underwear underneath her dress for the evening.

Few women would not enjoy being catered to, but if your girlfriend prefers the uncomplicated life, take her trekking and fiking in the wilderness. Choose a beautiful national park or hiking route, get as far away from civilization as you can, lay down a blanket or towel, and let loose in the wild! If you can, locate a lake or waterfall to go skinny diving in beforehand.

One final thought on pleasing your girlfriend

You will be pleased if she is happy. There's an old proverb that goes, "Happy wife, happy life." There aren't many things she won't be receptive to if you satisfy her sexual desires, at least in an effort to keep you satisfied in the bedroom.

42 Ways to Make a Lady Wet & Satisfied in Bed Just Thinking About You If you want to have a fantastic sexual life, you must learn how to make a woman feel satisfied in bed. She will be pleading with you for more if you follow these beautiful and steamy advice.

It takes more than just getting an orgasm to satisfy a lady in bed. It combines flexibility, emotion, and foreplay.

Giving your girlfriend what she wants won't be an issue for you if you know exactly what you're doing. Yet, there is a potential that your partner might be lying if you are unsure of your skills.

It only requires a deeper comprehension of your companion and her requirements.

Your sexual life will continue to be exciting and vibrant for a very long time as long as you prioritize your partner's sexual demands over your own, and remember to keep sex fresh.

Why satisfying a lady in bed is crucial

The "wham, bam, thank you ma'am" sexual ritual is sadly well-known among many guys. They are, in other words, self-centered. They only really care about enjoying themselves and having an orgasm.

But are you sure that would make a woman happy in bed? Do you honestly believe she is such a "giver" that she is unconcerned about her own wellbeing?

Obviously not!

Because it takes longer to turn on a woman than it does for him to get turned on, males often behave selfishly in bed. He doesn't believe she requires further stimulation since he believes her body responds just as swiftly as his does. Yet, she does.

And that's where most men become slothful. To satisfy a lady in bed and cause her to climax requires effort and a lot of "labor." But that doesn't make it challenging.

While some women are more amenable to pleasing than others, all of them deserve a partner who can satisfy their sexual needs.

In the bedroom, how long does it take to satisfy a woman?

Immediately is the response you are presumably hoping to hear. That's not the case, though. Women take longer to orgasm and become turned on than males, as was just mentioned. Also, what one lady enjoys, another may not.

Some women have a good understanding of their bodies and will go to any lengths to climax. Some people are completely unaware. That suggests that it might be possible to immediately please one woman. She might never feel completely happy with others. Thus, there isn't a simple solution to this problem. Just make the effort and observe her response to see how satisfied she appears to be at any particular time.

Sexual and emotional gratification

You should be aware that for women, emotional intimacy plays a significant role in determining sexual happiness.

Two individuals can get together and have fantastic sex for a while, after all. Nevertheless, boredom will quickly set in and the thrill of passionate sex will start to go away quickly.

Yet, if you know how to emotionally please a female, you can develop a stronger emotional bond with her and improve the quality of your long-term sex. Before implementing these sexual advice, read the introduction on how to please a lady both emotionally and sexually to improve your relationship.

How to make a woman happy in bed
The strongest sexual organ that humans have is not found in our underwear, despite what you may have previously heard. In our minds.

The brain is the part of your body that contributes the most to amazing sex, more so than any other part. The likelihood is high that every other area of your body will concur with your thinking if you are experiencing amazing sex.

You must first learn to make your partner's mind love what you do in bed in order to have absolutely fantastic sex and make her feel satisfied. Her body will follow after her intellect is enjoying it before her emotions do as well. There are numerous ways to please a woman if you are aware of it. Yet in order to do so, a particular set of requirements must be satisfied. Female orgasms are difficult to induce, especially when two individuals are just starting to get to know one another.

Some women are unable to even satisfy their own needs. How then can males expect to measure up if that is the case? If you get that correctly, she'll be more than satisfied. Guys can lose the erection very quickly and are sexually aroused very quickly. A woman, however, takes her time being aroused, and once she does, she maintains that state for a considerable amount of time.

Even if you've been in the same relationship for a very long time, you can still make a woman desire more of you by using these strategies to make her feel satisfied in bed.

1. Drop to her level

This generally works when all else fails. Go down on your woman and spend some delicate time down there if you're having trouble warming her up for the act.

This would almost always contribute to creating a terrific night.

2. Give foreplay some time

Most men rush through the foreplay portion without regard for the woman they are with. The fact that you are awake and prepared does not imply that your partner is as well. Both of you will enjoy sex a lot more if you take your time before penetration.

Different regimens are needed for various women. When it comes to foreplay, some women have predictable demands like kissing, licking, and stroking.

Some call for slightly more difficult procedures, such as synchronized undressing, role-playing, filthy conversation, hair pulling, etc. There are many options, but it's vital to know which one is ideal for both your partner and you.

3. Keep in mind her erogenous areas

A woman typically has multiple erogenous zones, ranging from the back of her neck, her ears, and all the way down to her knees and toes. Yet each woman has a few unique sweet places that instantly turn the button on.

Make sure you pay attention to the areas of her body that thrill her more than others as you kiss and nibble throughout the full length of her body. The next time you want to get her more excited quickly, it will always be useful.

4. Avoid dozing off on your back.

It's a positive indication if you fall asleep right after sex since it shows that your relationship is stable enough for you to just enjoy the calm after-sex feeling without worrying about unpleasant situations. The line between being safe and taking your lady for granted is thin, though. After sexual activity, cuddle or spend some time talking on your pillow. Maybe simply nod off while holding each other.

5. Your hygiene is important

The experience your wife has in bed is greatly influenced by how you present yourself. After all, isn't a more attractive mate more seductive? But keep in mind that being attractive doesn't only entail having six-pack abs.

If you're making love at the conclusion of a long day, take a shower and keep all those hairy areas neatly groomed. Your woman will find it difficult to take her hands off of you if you smell and feel amazing in bed.

6. Tell and kiss

Women tend to focus more on feelings than outward looks and have vivid imaginations. Use the proper words to arouse your woman's mind in order to turn her on and fulfill her in bed.

Discuss her favorite fantasy in private. She will experience an orgasm that will grab you tightly down there as long as you continue to intrigue her mind with your enticing phrases.

7. Avoid selfishness

This is as easy as it gets if you want to know how to satisfy a woman in bed. Prioritize your woman's needs before your own in bed.

Learn her preferences in bed, whether they are for low lighting or lying on the right side, and make sure she is at ease enough to enjoy having sex without any embarrassment or insecurities.

8. Always try new things.

The sexiest relationships are the ones where the partners simply follow the rules and don't experiment in any way, whether it be with positions or lewd remarks.

Do new things frequently if you want to achieve more than merely satisfying your partner in bed. Do something different to shake things up if you feel that a certain position or sex fantasy is starting to get boring.

9. The appropriate kudos

In bed, women adore being appreciated. They are able to let go of their inhibitions more readily and begin experimenting in bed sooner.

Make sure you tell your woman the amazing item you've discovered about her when you're both nude in bed together. She'll feel more confident in herself, which will result in greater sex.

10. Reactive areas and imaginations

Do any of your fantasies cause you to become uncomfortable the moment you think about them? Of course, girls also have trigger fantasies. It may be an erogenous zone for some girls, whilst for others it may be a sexual dream.

Find out what makes your woman turn on right away by talking to her. It'll play a significant role in arousing her, and occasionally, it can speed up the climax process if you can't hold on for too long.

11. Touch her body.

You shouldn't stop paying attention to the rest of her just because you're inside of her. Experiment with her body by touching her all over.

She was being massaged, rubbed, and grabbed all over. Your girl will be turned on much more than only by the missionary.

12. Always change up the sex

The main factor that makes sex monotonous after a while is that it can get fairly repetitious. The most cozy and intimate position of all may be the standard foreplay-followed-by-missionary-position sex. Try something new every so often, just to change things up in your bedroom.

Try playing pretend, using foul language, or playing a few erotic games in bed. Bring an intriguing twist into sex just as it begins to become predictable.

You can make every time you have sex with your woman feel like a one-night stand by constantly changing things up!

13. Suck, lick, and bite

Kissing is romantic and passionate. Don't stop there though. When you bite her and tongue her body, let her feel your desire.

And here's something to keep in mind: Even after dating for a while, a lady will still feel passionate about a good love bite in the right places.

Be outrageous in 14.

The more extravagant and crazy something feels, the sexier it feels. Learn to be risqué with your behavior if you want to gratify your woman. Sex will feel much more interesting if you sometimes do something risky.

Use blindfolds, have intercourse beside an open window, or grope each other on a dim dance floor... The intercourse will be more seductive the crazier your ideas and behaviors.

15. Her first erection

One of the best ways to please a woman in bed is to do this. The very last and most crucial piece of advice for pleasing your woman. The pinnacle of romantic endeavor is the ideal climax.

Also, it is almost probable that she won't get an orgasm if you do so before her. So that you can totally fulfill your woman before you climax, learn to control your erection and extend its duration.

16. The G-Spot

It's not that difficult to locate, but for some people, getting to it can be challenging. Every woman has a unique depth and level of sensitivity, making it challenging to achieve a g-spot orgasm.

Asking your partner what feels best for her in terms of speed, reach, and pressure is the best course of action.

17. The place

When it comes to the environment, women have varying preferences. While some prefer it in potentially dangerous locations like public restrooms, others want you to dress up your bedroom with roses and candles. Find out what she enjoys and, if you can, provide it to her.

18. Mood The setting, the food, or the conversation can all influence mood. Everything relies on how your first date or meeting goes.

Sensual foods like strawberries and chocolates might turn on certain ladies. Some people enjoy hearing about your plans for putting them in a good mood.

19. The time period

You can make a woman orgasm in 30 seconds if you're really skilled at what you do. Yet, this does not imply that one orgasm is sufficient.

Women like having several orgasms, and occasionally they even anticipate having several. In order to do that using your prowess in bed, you must be physically prepared.

20. The dance moves

Sometimes being a missionary is sufficient, but every now and then a lady might desire to try something new.

So that you can learn what she is willing to try the next time you sleep together, gently introduce your ideas into a conversation while you are in bed.

21. Self-assurance

You must appear to be knowledgeable about what you're doing. Nothing turns off a lady more quickly than a man who lacks control over his member or his hands.

Ask your friends for advice on how to please a woman if you want some practical advice. Do not be timid. That's what locker room talk is for.

22. Use sexting all day long

Do you recall how we said that sex begins in the mind? Well, women are particularly affected by this. Therefore, if you want some action in the evening, start by attempting to sext her.

Tell her what you want to do to her when you see her next and use sexy and flirtatious language. She'll become enthused by that and want to jump your bones.

23. Ask her what she wants in bed

Because a lot of men are selfish in bed, they don't ask the woman what she wants and what feels nice. This is partially because he's selfish and partially because of his ego

Many men erroneously believe themselves to be "The Greatest Lovers of All Time." Yet someone who truly deserves that label will inquire about their partner's desires and how they feel. He is, in other words, unselfish. And one of the best ways to please a woman in bed is by doing that.

24. Have fun with toys

Speaking of ego, when using toys, especially vibrators, you shouldn't let your ego get in the way.

Some women find it more harder to orgasm, and a lot of them require assistance. Don't let that or the other toys she wants to try make you feel threatened. She'll be grateful to you for it.

25. Use lubricant.

Not all females require lubrication. Some people are constantly wet by nature. But, some don't. You must therefore use some lubricant. Dry sex is not a pleasant experience for a woman. It feels bad and creates excessive friction. Even though a woman does naturally get wet, the more she dries up the longer you have sex. Have the lubrication on ready for her if you are a marathon man in bed.

26. Give the clitoris priority

The clitoris resembles the female penis in every way. Up to a certain time during fetal development, both boys and girls look alike. The same organ then either develops into the penis or the clitoris.

That is why it gives women such great pleasure. Most of them experience their orgasms there. Therefore pay close attention to that area.

27. Provide a sexy massage

Who doesn't enjoy a relaxing massage? It not only feels amazing, but it's even better coming from your nude sweetheart. Her brain and the rest of her body will be turned on if you give her an erotic massage.

Whilst you are massaging her, try using scented oils or perhaps some food. In order to build anticipation and make her desire you more, touch her in all the right areas and tease her just enough.

28. Be in touch before, during, and after

You likely already know that ladies enjoy talking. Many women don't appreciate it when men keep their mouths silent during sex, despite the fact that most men do. Talk to her before, during, and following your intercourse, then. She'll feel more a part of you.

29. Maintain a tidy bed

Unfortunately, many men don't make the best housekeepers. Many of them may neglect washing their bed linens for several months.

But, the majority of women find that utterly repugnant. So that she won't be afraid to climb into the bed, do your clothes and keep food and pets away from it.

30. Let her to take charge

Not all ladies enjoy being obedient in bed. Many women enjoy being in charge, if not always then frequently.

Hence, inquire as to her desire to assume charge and when. Let her know that she has complete control over you, and then do as she directs.

31. Take your time taking off each other's clothing.

Yeah, we are aware that once you are turned on and aware that you will engage in sex, you want to go right to the enjoyable parts. For women, however, making out, kissing, and fondling while wearing clothing is a big part of the "good stuff."

Thus, act like you two are teenagers and take your time having sexual relations. Enjoy each moment and take your time. That's a fantastic method to make a woman happy before you make love to her.

32. Speak softly in her ear

If you whisper sexy things in a woman's ear during sex, she will always be turned on. You might congratulate her on her appearance or the sexual acts she performs on you. Perhaps you might just sigh and tell her how wonderful it is or how wonderful it feels to have her body on yours.

33. using your fingers

We don't just mean to finger her when we say "fingers." Yes, a few females actually enjoy that. But, some don't.

Fingers can be used anywhere on the body. from her clit to her nipples. Thus, don't forget to include them anytime you feel like it.

34. Treat her gently

Many women enjoy tender, sweet, and emotional sex. You must therefore treat her body with care. Certainly, some people might enjoy it being tough and rough, but the majority don't.

You don't want to damage her by accident, so be gentle with her body. That doesn't turn me on.

35. After you both finish, don't forget to hug her.

Women are emotional, so even after the physical act of having sex has ended, they still believe the experience hasn't ended.

Don't forget to do that since they view afterplay, which includes cuddling and pillow conversation, as an extension of it. That demonstrates to her that you care about more than just her physical appearance.

How to determine whether she is content in bed

There are other, more reliable ways for you to determine whether you were able to satisfy your lover in bed besides moaning or shouting. It's better if you don't even have to ask her, though.

1. She looks

During her amorously satiated state, gaze into her eyes and utter sweet nothings. Check to see if she has dilated pupils while you're doing that. She has just experienced an orgasm, as evidenced by that.

2. PC muscles

Women who are having orgasms have far stronger PC muscle contractions. You can tell whether your penis is contracting on its own accord or as a result of an orgasm if you pay close attention to the feelings it is experiencing. Orgasmic contractions typically have stronger contractions.

3. She is tired.

After some sex, if all she does is lay down and then falls asleep next to you like a baby, you know you did the job.

Unexpectedly, experiencing an orgasm requires more energy than initiating one. Men and women both desire to sleep right away after having sex for this reason.

4. Trembling

A genuine shudder cannot be manufactured; yet, it is highly noticeable. You can be certain that a lady is experiencing an orgasm if she shivers both during and after.

A real shiver makes her appear as though she went outside nude in the snow while a false shiver is typically languid and weak.

5. She mutters

Stop base women's true orgasm moans on porn, boys. Such gals are actresses (occasionally not very good ones), and they exaggerate for the benefit of the camera.

If a woman is genuinely experiencing an orgasm, she may gasp, mumble, scream, moan, or groan as an animal might. She cannot practice it till she has received an Oscar Award.

6. The way she breathed

If a girl decides to keep quiet during sex, you can infer things from the way she breathes and gasps during and after an orgasm. A girl will arrive and breathe heavily, fiercely, profoundly, and slowly.

After she is finished, she will exhale fast, deeply, and forcefully as if she had just completed a marathon. After a few seconds, this will abruptly slow down, and at that point you will know that she is content.

7. You cannot handle it

A woman will no longer allow you to touch her clitoris after an orgasm. You can try, but her body won't withstand it because her climax made it extremely sensitive.

The same thing happens when guys orgasm. After an orgasm, you cannot over stimulate the penis and continue.

Be vigilant and observant to make the most of these suggestions. These are subtle indications that cannot be quickly identified. Keep an eye on your partner for indications that they might be lying. It can be appropriate for you to discuss it if you feel that you failed to please them.

As long as you keep in mind these pointers for pleasing a lady in bed, maintaining a woman's sexual satisfaction isn't actually all that difficult. If you keep them in mind, your girl will be overjoyed with your bedroom abilities.

Understanding a woman's wishes and emotional requirements is crucial to satisfying her in bed. Keep in mind that foreplay is always essential to arousing her, so make sure to kiss, caress, and examine her body.

When she becomes aroused, you should watch for her body language and follow her cues for what feels right for her. You can always make your woman happy in bed if you are ready to be patient and concentrate on her pleasure.

Sexual orientation

Who you are attracted to and want to be in relationships with determines your sexual orientation. Gay, lesbian, straight, bisexual, and asexual are the different sexual orientations.

Gender and gender identity are distinct from sexual orientation.

Sexual orientation refers to the people you are emotionally, romantically, and sexually drawn to. It's not the same as gender identity. Gender identification refers to who you ARE – male, female, genderqueer, etc. — rather than who you are attracted to.

As a result, being transgender—feeling as though the gender you identify with is very different from the sex you were assigned—is distinct from being gay, lesbian, or bisexual. What matters in sexual orientation is who you want to be with. The question of gender identification is personal.

Numerous identities are connected to sexual orientation, including:

Individuals who are attracted to a different gender, such as men or women who are drawn to women, may identify as straight or heterosexual.

The terms "gay" or "homosexual" are frequently used by people who are attracted to other people of the same gender. Lesbian may be preferred by gay women.

Individuals who have feelings for both men and women frequently identify as bisexuals.

Pansexual or queer individuals are those who find themselves attracted to people of many different gender identities, including male, female, transgender, gender queer, intersex, etc.

Individuals who are unsure about their sexual orientation may describe themselves as curious or unsure.

Those who don't feel any sexual desire toward someone commonly identify as asexual.

Furthermore noteworthy is the fact that some individuals feel none of these designations adequately describe them. Some people have strong opposition to the concept of labels. Certain designations are acceptable to some people while not others. You get to choose how, if at all, you wish to label yourself.

Queer: What does that mean?

Diverse sexual orientations and gender identities that are not straight and cisgender are referred to as queer.

The term "queer" was once used to injure and deride others. Some people still find it insulting, especially those who are still sensitive to the way the word was once used. Some now proudly self-identify with the word.

If you don't know how they identify themselves, you might not want to call them "queer." Use their language while discussing their sexual orientation with others. Asking about people's preferred labels is acceptable (and frequently encouraged!).

Asexuality: What is it?

Asexual people don't actually experience sexual attraction to anyone. They may find other individuals to be physically alluring or desire romantic connections with them, but they are not interested in engaging in sexual activity with them. Asexual people occasionally abbreviate words with "ace."

Romantic attraction has nothing to do with asexuality. Many asexual people experience romantic attraction toward others, leading them to self-identify as both asexual and homosexual, lesbian, bisexual, or straight. They simply lack the willingness to act sexually on these feelings.

Like everyone else, asexual folks have emotional needs. While some asexuals are interested in romantic relationships, others are not. Apart than sex, they establish intimacy or closeness with others.

Some individuals who identify as aromantic do not experience romantic attraction or desire romantic partnerships. Being asexual and being aromantic are two different things.

While some asexuals are aroused (turned on), they lack the desire to engage in sexual activity with others. Also, some asexuals engage in masturbation. Others, however, might not experience any arousal at all.

Although though it's very natural to have periods of time when you don't want to have sex, this does not necessarily indicate that you are an asexual. Asexuality is not the same as celibacy, either. Asexuality is a sexual identity that comes naturally to you, whereas celibacy is a decision you make.

Asexuality, like other sexual orientations, isn't usually clear-cut. Between being sexual (having a sexual desire) and being asexual, there is a range. Individuals fall into several categories throughout that spectrum. Some people who don't find other people sexually attractive identify as gray-a. Some persons who only experience sexual attraction to others with whom they are in committed relationships self-identify as demisexual. Interested in learning how someone identifies? Query them.

There is nothing "wrong" with persons who are asexual, and there is no proof that this is due to poor mental health or trauma of any type. It's actually rather prevalent; according to some studies, 1 in 100 persons identify as asexual. The Asexual Visibility and Education Network has further details on asexuality.

What if I object to being classified?

It's acceptable if you don't want to carry a label. Only you know which sexual identity most accurately defines you. Nonetheless, some individuals could feel that none of the popular designations feel accurate to them.

Your sexual identity and orientation can stay the same over the course of your life. Maybe it might change based on the person you're attracted to, in a romantic relationship with, or engaging in sexual activity. This is entirely typical. There is no reason why a title you've given yourself can't evolve as you do.

You are not "confused" if you change how you identify. Many people, both young and old, go through changes in their identity and the people they are drawn to. We refer to this as "fluidity."

What Is Sexual anxiety

A fear-based reaction to sex and/or closeness is sexual anxiety. It frequently prevents intercourse and can take over a person's psychological, physical, and emotional state. There are numerous factors that might affect sexual anxiety before, during, and after sexual activity. Men could worry about their sexual performance, and women might worry about their partner's approval or their level of desire.

It's common to experience some anticipation or even trepidation before having sex. The feeling of anticipation you experience while trying out a new sex item with a long-term spouse or getting butterflies before having sex with a new partner are not the same as sexual anxiety.

How Worry Can Impair Your Sexual Life

Negative physiological and psychological states, such as sexual frustration, are frequently experienced by people who struggle with sexual anxiety. This frequently leads to unfavorable thoughts before, during, and after sex, which increases anxiety or fear. It can be challenging to remain present and in the moment when anxiety takes over. The battle to "get in the mood" can then result in emotions of failure or guilt. Occasionally these emotions can get so strong that a person decides to stay away from them and stops having sex entirely.

Having sex may help with the symptoms of anxiety in those who have been diagnosed with a disorder of anxiety unrelated to sex and intimacy. Yet, if anti-anxiety medications are administered to aid with symptoms, they may be at risk of developing sexual anxiety due to a decreased sex drive. Benzodiazepines, such as Valium, Xanax, and Ativan, and SSRIs, such as Prozac, Zoloft, Lexapro, and Effexor, are the two main types of drugs used to treat anxiety disorders.2 These drugs frequently work brilliantly in treating anxiety symptoms, but they frequently have the unwanted side effect of decreasing sex drive in addition to other undesirable effects including weight gain.

Sex anxiety signs and symptoms

Physical sensations like a stomach ache, a racing heartbeat, or a sense of dread surrounding the prospect of sex and/or closeness may also be present in people with sexual anxiety. These intrusive thoughts or worries can also be experienced by those with sexual anxiety.

3 Moreover, they can be suffering with sexual dysfunction, sexual avoidance, or sexual performance anxiety.

Fear of sexual performance

An individual may feel sexual performance anxiety when they are under stress and have unfavorable thoughts about their sexual performance. Penis size, body image, relationship issues, and other outside pressures can all exacerbate feelings of inadequacy. Sexual performance anxiety frequently develops at the beginning of a relationship, but if it worsens or last for more than three months, it may be time to consult a physician to rule out any underlying medical conditions.

Dysfunctional Sexuality

An individual who suffers from sexual dysfunction finds it difficult to enjoy their sexual encounters. It can happen at any stage of the sexual response cycle and is a frequent yet taboo topic that isn't often acknowledged. 4 The phases of the sexual response cycle are: stimulation, plateau, orgasm, and resolution. It's crucial to note that women don't always follow these phases in exact order. These phases contain both arousal and desire.

Desire disorders, arousal disorders, orgasm disorders, and pain disorders are the four basic categories of sexual dysfunction.

4 Men and women alike may feel uninterested in sex, have trouble getting aroused, and feel pain during intercourse. Additionally, there are signs that are specific to men only, such as failure to ejaculate or premature ejaculation, as well as problems achieving and maintaining an erection. Inability to orgasm, dryness of the vagina before and during intercourse, and inability to relax the vaginal muscles during intercourse are a few symptoms that are specific to women (vaginismus). 3

Sexual dysfunction can be brought on by a variety of physical (health conditions, excessive alcohol or drug use, or prescription drugs) or psychological factors (stress, depression, anxiety, or trauma).

4 Always consult a medical expert to identify the root of any sexual problems and choose the most appropriate course of action.

Sexual Abstaining

Many people may avoid dating, intimacy, relationships, and sex if their dread and worries about sex cause them to experience extremely high levels of anxiety. This may begin as a defense mechanism but can escalate into more extreme sexual avoidance, in which people avoid having sex to avoid feeling any discomfort associated with their body image, performance, or past trauma. 5 Sexual avoidance behaviors can be identified and treated with expert anxiety-reduction therapies.

What Leads to Sexual Panic?

Sexual anxiety can have many distinct causes, and they normally vary from person to person. An increase in sex anxiety may be observed in those dealing with mental health disorders, trauma, and numerous relationship problems. Moreover, anxiety is frequently cyclical, and people frequently struggle to restrain their worry. 1

Psychological Health Issues

Factors affecting mental health significantly affect quality of life. Many people find that while trying to be intimate with a partner, their body image and sense of self-consciousness can undermine their confidence and self-esteem. High levels of stress and worry from job, family, or daily life can also cause issues in the bedroom. Fortunately, discussing these areas of concern with a specialist can benefit mental health. Making healthy lifestyle adjustments can also enhance mental health. They include getting enough sleep, eating wholesome, balanced meals, and exercising.

Encounters with trauma in the past

Those who have experienced sexual trauma in the past frequently struggle to normalize any sexual experience when they join a relationship. tragic events from the past and a relationship Flashbacks, disturbing recollections, or avoidance may be signs of PTSD in new romantic relationships. 3 A trauma survivor can process the traumatic incident and then discover coping mechanisms to deal with stressful situations and anxiety-inducing situations through the establishment of a strong therapeutic connection.

Problems in Relationships

Intimacy concerns can also affect relationships. Problems with or a lack of communication in a relationship, which may include an increase in fighting or disputing without resolution, a fear of intimacy, and compatibility concerns are some of the things that are crucial to watch out for. For each of these factors, communication is essential. Although it could seem intimidating to bring up the subject with your significant other, keeping these problems hidden may make you feel more anxious. A solution to reestablishing communication and enhancing the partnership is couples counselling.

How to Recognize the Sources of Your Sexual Anxiety

Try to become curious about what you're feeling without placing blame or judgment on it in order to begin discovering your triggers for sexual anxiety. Keep a note of the times when the feelings arise, and then attempt to trace their origin. It can begin with a difficult day at work during which you feel underappreciated, and it might then spill over into the bedroom. It might also be the result of a particular memory that was awakened in the past. It's crucial to discuss your triggers with your partner when you've identified them. Be honest about your struggles and how you think you can be supported.

Options for Treating Anxiety

Consult a therapist who is qualified in talk therapy. Online counselling is available from Betterhelp starting at $60 per week. Get a Therapist match

Virtual Psychiatry: Find a real doctor who accepts your insurance and receive help. Talkiatry provides online consultations with renowned psychiatrists as well as medication management. Take the online evaluation, then schedule your initial visit for the following week. Free Evaluation

Choosing Therapy collaborates with top mental health businesses and receives payment from Better Help and Talkiatry for marketing.

7 Ways to Manage Sexual Anxiety

While having to deal with sexual anxiety can seem overwhelming, there are a number of methods you can take to assist get over those emotions. Being secretive about your anxiety could end up causing additional avoidance, so it's crucial to be open with both yourself and your partner.

The following are seven methods for overcoming sex anxiety:

1. Engage in mind fullness

Try grounding yourself by concentrating on your breath or other physical sensations rather than paying attention to any anxiety, fear, or worry that arises.

2. Emphasis on Masturbation and Self-Touch

Investigating self-touch can boost libido and give one a sense of empowerment.

6 This might lessen the connection between sex and worry and foster more positive attitudes regarding sex.

3. Describe Your Favorites and Dislikes

By using self-touch to identify your triggers, you may then openly and assertively communicate with your spouse about what you've learnt. Sayings like "I'd like it if you would try to touch me here instead" can be used to accomplish this.

4. Decrease Stress

In addition to sexual anxiety, it may be beneficial to pay attention to the source of your elevated emotions of stress in other areas of your life. To help manage your life stress, make sure you are getting enough sleep each night, eating wholesome foods, and exercising frequently. You could find that doing this makes your anxiety feel more manageable in all facets of your life.

5. Put your partner's connection first.

The key to sexual intimacy is building a connection with your partner. Building a secure and close relationship with an emphasis on exploration is the ultimate goal rather than necessarily engaging in sexual activity or experiencing orgasm.

6. Talk to others

No matter how challenging or painful it may be, it's crucial to express what you're feeling. Finding solutions that work for you both means discussing your problems with your partner, as well as how your needs and preferences have changed. Regular check-ins are necessary for healthy sex communication to ensure that you are both on the same page and moving toward the same objectives.

7. Concentrate on Intimacy & Erogenous Zones Without Sex Pressure

Erogenous zones are parts of the body that can be aroused and are responsive to touch. A study found that stimulation of non genital erogenous zones can cause orgasms in 12% of women. 7 Each has a unique experience with the many erogenous zones. The lips, ears, neck, breasts, and inner thighs are a few of the most typical erogenous zones. The scalp, inner wrist, navel, and calves are a few that are less well known but nonetheless helpful. 8 There are various ways to activate the erogenous zones, including gentle touching, breathing on the region, using the tongue and mouth, or using sex toys.

Locate a friendly therapist who can help you overcome your sexual phobia. More than 20,000 licensed therapists are available for quick and inexpensive online treatment through Better Help. Better Help's weekly rate is $60. Fill out a short form to be matched with the best therapist.

Choosing Therapy collaborates with top mental health businesses and is paid by Better Help for marketing.

Access Better Help

Get Expert Assistance for Sexual Anxiety

It may be time to consult a professional if you have tried these methods or have gone through a terrible incident but are still experiencing anxiety. To rule out a medical problem or a side effect from a drug, it is a good idea to first consult with your doctor. Sex therapy is an additional choice for addressing the sexual issues in a relationship. A simple and successful alternative is sensate focus sex therapy, which uses structured touching exercises to promote intimacy and connection between a couple. It might be risky, but also extremely beneficial, to seek professional assistance.

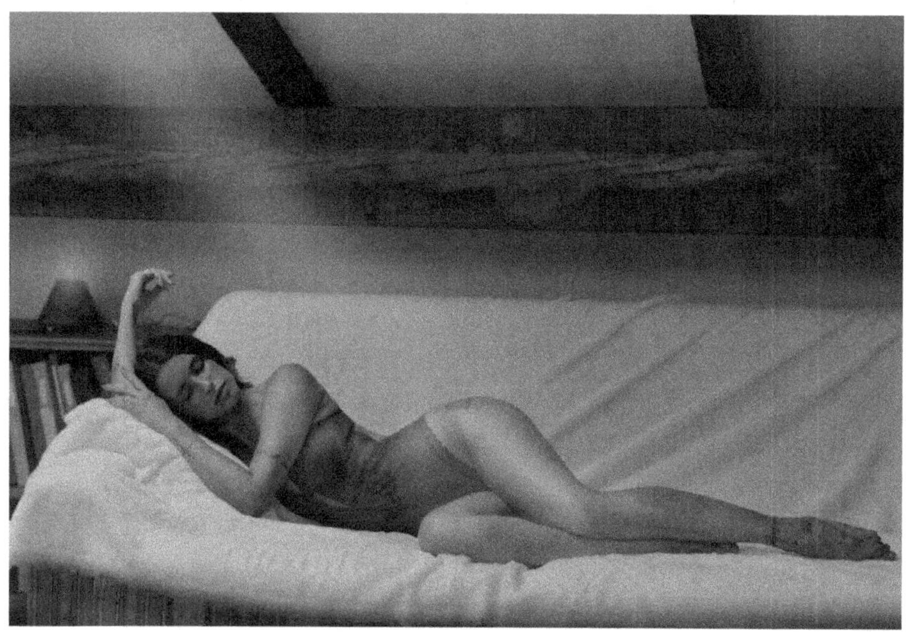

How to Help a Spouse Who Is Sexually Anxious

Many worries and feelings can surface when a partner is dealing with sexual anxiety. It's crucial to exercise compassion and patience. Even if you don't fully get what your spouse is going through, practice listening to your partner in order to collaborate and find answers. Also, it will help to create a comfortable environment that encourages intimacy if there is open and honest conversation without any sense of shame or guilt.

Focus on acting in a way that feels good as you learn to manage your sexual anxieties. Hand holding, embraces, kisses, and other types of physical contact that don't entail penetration are just a few examples. Couples can also attempt staying in the present moment with one another by leaning into their sense of touch, scent, and hearing instead of getting caught up in concerns or worries. Even while getting over sexual anxiety in a partnership can seem like a difficult endeavor, when handled jointly, it can be a means to fortify and enhance a connection.

Final Reflections

In a relationship, it can be challenging to overcome sexual anxiety, but it can be controlled with open communication and honesty. Partnerships are about cultivating a connection, which may be accomplished by prioritizing developing a secure and nourishing intimate relationship. Focusing on connection and intimacy will assist create a safe and enjoyable encounter by removing the fear and anxiety from sex.

Sexual Issues and Their Solutions

Firstly, impotence

When a man cannot achieve or maintain an erection, this condition is also referred to as impotence. It affects the majority of males at some point in their lives, and its reasons might be either psychological or physical.

(2) Early ejaculation

It occurs when a man ejaculates during intercourse before he intends to. Only if it affects him or his companion is it a problem. Stress, unresolved relationship troubles, concern about sexual performance, and depression can all be contributing factors.

3. Delay in Ejaculation

Long-term health issues, adverse drug reactions, alcoholism, or surgical procedures are a few examples. Psychological variables including despair, anxiety, stress, or relationship issues might also contribute to this issue.

4. Limited Libido

Reduced libido indicates a decline in sex-related interest or desire. Low levels of the male hormone testosterone are a contributing factor in the illness. Muscle, hair, bone, and sperm production are all maintained. Your body and mood might be impacted by low testosterone. Depression, anxiety, or interpersonal connection issues can all lead to decreased sexual inclinations. Low libido can also be brought on by diabetes, hypertension, and some drugs like antidepressants.

Solutions

Most sexual dysfunction instances can be resolved by attending to the underlying medical or psychological issues.

Medical Care: This entails treating any medical issues that might be causing a man's sexual dysfunction.

Via Drugs: By boosting blood flow to the penis, medications like Cialis, Levitra, Staxyn, Stendra, or Viagra may help men with erectile dysfunction. It (Promescent) is a medication for the treatment of early ejaculation. The lidocaine-containing spray is used on the penis to reduce sensitivity and improve ejaculation control. They are only short-term fixes for sexual issues.

Psychological Therapy: Counseling is provided by a qualified and experienced counselor and aids a person in addressing feelings of worry, fear, or guilt that can affect their ability to conceive.

Implants: Erectile dysfunction treatment options for men include penile implants and vacuum devices. But, you should be aware that talking to a doctor about your sexual issues and potential solutions is also a good idea!

Communication and Education

Discuss sex and sexual actions and reactions. It might assist a man in getting over his concerns about sexual performance. Honest communication about desires and concerns with the partner also aids in removing many obstacles to healthy sex life.

According to research, 31% of men and 43% of women experience some level of difficulties with sexual dysfunction. Many people are reluctant to talk about sexual problems and solutions. Luckily, most sexual dysfunction cases can be resolved. So, it's crucial to discuss your worries with your spouse and doctor. You can contact us by Whatsapp (+91 9654030724) or email at connect@gomedii.com to learn more about our services and to get an immediate appointment or consultation for Sexual Issues. We will respond to you as soon as we can.

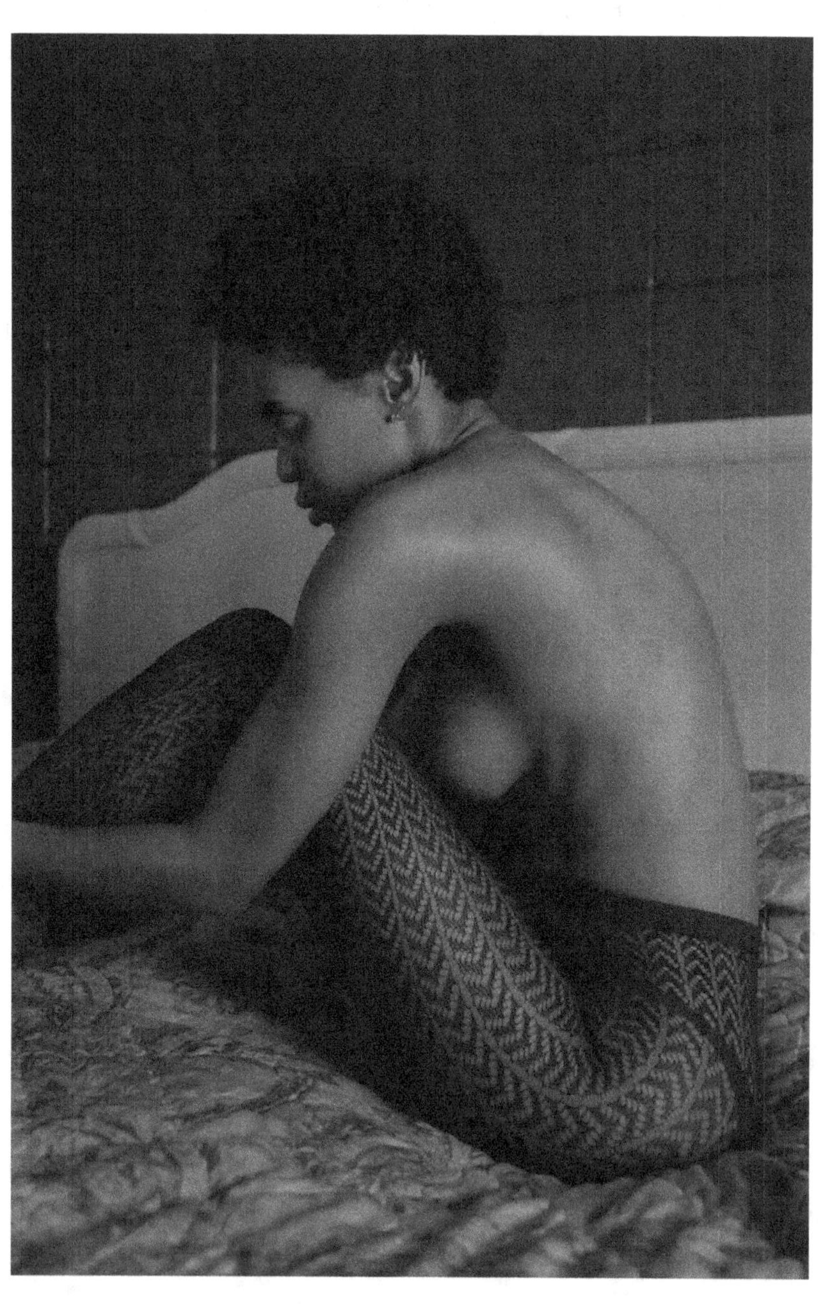

Conclusion

The book of sexual satisfaction is a comprehensive guide that delves deep into the intricacies of human sexuality and provides readers with practical tips and advice on how to enhance their sexual experiences. The book covers a wide range of topics, from the basics of sexual anatomy and physiology to the psychology of sexual desire and the art of seduction.

One of the key takeaways from the book is that sexual satisfaction is not just about physical pleasure but also about emotional and psychological fulfillment. The authors emphasize the importance of communication, trust, and intimacy in building a strong and healthy sexual relationship.

The book also highlights the importance of exploring one's own sexuality and understanding one's own needs and desires. Through self-exploration and experimentation, individuals can discover new ways of experiencing pleasure and improve their overall sexual satisfaction.

Another important theme of the book is the role of cultural and societal factors in shaping our attitudes and beliefs about sex. The authors encourage readers to challenge traditional gender roles and stereotypes and to embrace diversity and inclusivity in their sexual relationships.

Overall, the book of sexual satisfaction is a valuable resource for anyone looking to improve their sexual experiences and enhance their overall well-being. By providing practical advice, insights, and strategies for building strong and fulfilling sexual relationships, the book empowers readers to take control of their own sexual lives and find greater satisfaction and happiness.

Moreover, the book emphasizes the importance of consent and mutual respect in sexual encounters. It provides guidance on how to communicate effectively with sexual partners and how to establish boundaries that are comfortable for everyone involved. The authors also discuss important topics such as sexual health, contraception, and sexual dysfunction, providing readers with the information they need to make informed decisions about their sexual health and well-being.

One of the strengths of the book is its accessibility. The authors use clear and concise language, making complex topics easy to understand for readers of all backgrounds and experience levels. The book is also well-organized, with each chapter building on the previous one to provide a comprehensive overview of sexual satisfaction.

In conclusion, the book of sexual satisfaction is a must-read for anyone interested in improving their sexual experiences and relationships. By providing practical advice and insights, the authors empower readers to take control of their sexual lives and find greater fulfillment and happiness. The book is a valuable resource for individuals, couples, and healthcare professionals, and is sure to make a positive impact on the lives of those who read it.